ELIZABETH II

Education (Schools) Act 1992

1992 CHAPTER 38

An Act to make provision with respect to the inspection of schools and with respect to information about schools and their pupils. [16th March 1992]

BE IT ENACTED by the Queen's most Excellent Majesty, by and with the advice and consent of the Lords Spiritual and Temporal, and Commons, in this present Parliament assembled, and by the authority of the same, as follows:—

Her Majesty's Inspectorate for England

1.—(1) Her Majesty may by Order in Council appoint a person to the office of Her Majesty's Chief Inspector of Schools in England ("the Chief Inspector for England").

(2) Her Majesty may by Order in Council appoint persons as Her Majesty's Inspectors of Schools in England.

(3) Any person appointed as one of Her Majesty's Inspectors of Schools in England shall serve, in accordance with the terms and conditions on which he is appointed, as a member of the staff of the Chief Inspector for England.

(4) The Chief Inspector for England shall hold and vacate office in accordance with the terms of his appointment, but—

    (a) shall not be appointed for a term of more than five years;

    (b) may at any time resign by giving written notice to the Secretary of State;

    (c) may be removed from office by Her Majesty on the ground of incapacity or misconduct.

(5) The previous appointment of a person as Chief Inspector for England shall not affect his eligibility for re-appointment.

(6) Schedule 1 makes further provision with respect to the Chief Inspector for England and his staff.

Her Majesty's Inspectorate of Schools in England.

Functions of the
Chief Inspector
for England.

2.—(1) The Chief Inspector for England shall have the general duty of keeping the Secretary of State informed about—

(a) the quality of the education provided by schools in England;

(b) the educational standards achieved in those schools;

(c) whether the financial resources made available to those schools are managed efficiently; and

(d) the spiritual, moral, social and cultural development of pupils at those schools.

(2) When asked to do so by the Secretary of State, the Chief Inspector for England shall—

(a) give advice to the Secretary of State on such matters as may be specified in the Secretary of State's request;

(b) inspect and report on such school, or class of school, in England as may be so specified.

(3) The Chief Inspector for England shall, in addition, have the following specific duties—

(a) establishing and maintaining the register mentioned in section 10(1);

(b) giving guidance to inspectors registered in that register, and such other persons as he considers appropriate, in connection with inspections of schools in England under section 9 and the making of reports of such inspections;

(c) keeping under review the system of inspecting schools under section 9 (so far as it relates to schools in England) and, in particular, the standard of such inspections and of the reports made by registered inspectors;

(d) keeping under review the extent to which any requirement imposed by or under this Act, or any other enactment, on any registered inspector, local education authority, proprietor of a school or governing body in relation to inspections of schools in England is complied with;

(e) promoting efficiency in the conduct and reporting of inspections of schools in England by encouraging competition in the provision of services by registered inspectors.

(4) The Chief Inspector for England may at any time give advice to the Secretary of State on any matter connected with schools, or a particular school, in England.

(5) The Chief Inspector for England shall have such other functions in connection with schools in England, including functions with respect to the training of teachers for such schools, as may be assigned to him by the Secretary of State.

(6) In exercising his functions the Chief Inspector for England shall have regard to such aspects of government policy as the Secretary of State may direct.

Power of Chief
Inspector for
England to
arrange for
inspections.

3.—(1) The Chief Inspector for England may cause any school in England to be inspected by one or more of Her Majesty's Inspectors of Schools in England (in this section referred to as "Inspectors").

Education (Schools) Act 1992

CHAPTER 38

ARRANGEMENT OF SECTIONS

(2) Where an inspection of a school in England is being conducted by a registered inspector under section 9, the Chief Inspector for England may arrange for that inspection to be monitored by one or more Inspectors.

(3) Any Inspector inspecting a school, or monitoring an inspection, under this section shall have at all reasonable times—

(a) a right of entry to the premises of the school; and

(b) a right to inspect, and take copies of, any records kept by the school, and any other documents containing information relating to the school, which he considers relevant to the discharge of his functions.

(4) It shall be an offence wilfully to obstruct any Inspector in the exercise of any of his functions under this section.

(5) A person guilty of an offence under subsection (4) shall be liable on summary conviction to a fine not exceeding level four on the standard scale.

4. The Chief Inspector for England—

(a) shall make an annual report to the Secretary of State, who shall lay a copy of it before each House of Parliament;

(b) may make such other reports to the Secretary of State, with respect to matters which fall within the scope of his functions, as he considers appropriate; and

(c) may arrange for any report made by him under this section to be published in such manner as he considers appropriate.

Annual and other reports of the Chief Inspector for England.

Her Majesty's Inspectorate for Wales

5.—(1) Her Majesty may by Order in Council appoint a person to the office of Her Majesty's Chief Inspector of Schools in Wales ("the Chief Inspector for Wales").

Her Majesty's Inspectorate of Schools in Wales.

(2) Her Majesty may by Order in Council appoint persons as Her Majesty's Inspectors of Schools in Wales.

(3) Any person appointed as one of Her Majesty's Inspectors of Schools in Wales shall serve, in accordance with the terms and conditions on which he is appointed, as a member of the staff of the Chief Inspector for Wales.

(4) The Chief Inspector for Wales shall hold and vacate office in accordance with the terms of his appointment, but—

(a) shall not be appointed for a term of more than five years;

(b) may at any time resign by giving written notice to the Secretary of State;

(c) may be removed from office by Her Majesty on the ground of incapacity or misconduct.

(5) The previous appointment of a person as Chief Inspector for Wales shall not affect his eligibility for re-appointment.

(6) Schedule 1 makes further provision with respect to the Chief Inspector for Wales and his staff.

Functions of the
Chief Inspector
for Wales.

6.—(1) The Chief Inspector for Wales shall have the general duty of keeping the Secretary of State informed about—

(a) the quality of the education provided by schools in Wales;

(b) the educational standards achieved in those schools;

(c) whether the financial resources made available to those schools are managed efficiently; and

(d) the spiritual, moral, social and cultural development of pupils at those schools.

(2) When asked to do so by the Secretary of State, the Chief Inspector for Wales shall—

(a) give advice to the Secretary of State on such matters as may be specified in the Secretary of State's request;

(b) inspect and report on such school, or class of school, in Wales as may be so specified.

(3) The Chief Inspector for Wales shall, in addition, have the following specific duties—

(a) establishing and maintaining the register mentioned in section 10(2);

(b) giving guidance to inspectors registered in that register, and such other persons as he considers appropriate, in connection with inspections of schools in Wales under section 9 and the making of reports of such inspections;

(c) keeping under review the system of inspecting schools under section 9 (so far as it relates to schools in Wales) and, in particular, the standard of such inspections and of the reports made by registered inspectors;

(d) keeping under review the extent to which any requirement imposed by or under this Act, or any other enactment, on any registered inspector, local education authority, proprietor of a school or governing body in relation to inspections of schools in Wales is complied with;

(e) promoting efficiency in the conduct and reporting of inspections of schools in Wales by encouraging competition in the provision of services by registered inspectors.

(4) The Chief Inspector for Wales may at any time give advice to the Secretary of State on any matter connected with schools, or a particular school, in Wales.

(5) The Chief Inspector for Wales shall have such other functions in connection with schools in Wales, including functions with respect to the training of teachers for such schools, as may be assigned to him by the Secretary of State.

(6) In exercising his functions the Chief Inspector for Wales shall have regard to such aspects of government policy as the Secretary of State may direct.

Power of Chief
Inspector for
Wales to arrange
for inspections.

7.—(1) The Chief Inspector for Wales may cause any school in Wales to be inspected by one or more of Her Majesty's Inspectors of Schools in Wales (in this section referred to as "Inspectors").

(2) Where an inspection of a school in Wales is being conducted by a registered inspector under section 9, the Chief Inspector for Wales may arrange for that inspection to be monitored by one or more Inspectors.

(3) Any Inspector inspecting a school, or monitoring an inspection, under this section shall have at all reasonable times—

(a) a right of entry to the premises of the school; and

(b) a right to inspect, and take copies of, any records kept by the school, and any other documents containing information relating to the school, which he considers relevant to the discharge of his functions.

(4) It shall be an offence wilfully to obstruct any Inspector in the exercise of any of his functions under this section.

(5) A person guilty of an offence under subsection (4) shall be liable on summary conviction to a fine not exceeding level four on the standard scale.

8. The Chief Inspector for Wales—

Annual and other reports of the Chief Inspector for Wales.

(a) shall make an annual report to the Secretary of State, who shall lay a copy of it before each House of Parliament;

(b) may make such other reports to the Secretary of State, with respect to matters which fall within the scope of his functions, as he considers appropriate; and

(c) may arrange for any report made by him under this section to be published in such manner as he considers appropriate.

Inspections by registered inspectors

9.—(1) It shall be the duty of the Chief Inspector for England to secure that every school in England to which this section applies is inspected, at such intervals as may be prescribed, by an inspector registered under section 10(1).

Inspection of certain schools.

(2) It shall be the duty of the Chief Inspector for Wales to secure that every school in Wales to which this section applies is inspected, at such intervals as may be prescribed, by an inspector registered under section 10(2).

(3) The schools to which this section applies are—

(a) county schools;

(b) voluntary schools;

(c) special schools;

(d) grant-maintained schools;

(e) independent schools approved by the Secretary of State under section 11(3)(a) of the Education Act 1981 (schools suitable for children for whom statements are maintained under section 7 of that Act);

1981 c. 60.

(f) city technology colleges;

(g) city colleges for the technology of the arts;

(h) maintained nursery schools.

(4) It shall be the general duty of any registered inspector conducting an inspection under this section to report on—

(a) the quality of the education provided by the school;

(b) the educational standards achieved in the school;

(c) whether the financial resources made available to the school are managed efficiently; and

(d) the spiritual, moral, social and cultural development of pupils at the school.

(5) In prescribing the intervals mentioned in subsections (1) and (2) the Secretary of State may make provision as to the period within which the first inspection of a school under this section is to begin.

(6) An inspection which is required under this section shall not extend to denominational education.

(7) Part I of Schedule 2 makes further provision with respect to inspections under this section.

Registration of inspectors.   **10.**—(1) No person shall conduct an inspection of any school in England under section 9(1) unless he is registered as an inspector in a register kept by the Chief Inspector for England for the purposes of this Act.

(2) No person shall conduct an inspection of any school in Wales under section 9(2) unless he is registered as an inspector in a register kept by the Chief Inspector for Wales for the purposes of this Act.

(3) The Chief Inspector shall not register a person under this section unless, having regard to any conditions that he proposes to impose under subsection (5)(c), it appears to him that that person—

(a) is a fit and proper person for discharging the functions of a registered inspector; and

(b) will be capable of conducting inspections under this Act competently and effectively.

(4) An application for registration under this section—

(a) shall be made in such manner, and be accompanied by such particulars, as the Chief Inspector may direct; and

(b) shall be accompanied by the prescribed fee.

(5) On an application duly made under this section the Chief Inspector may—

(a) register the applicant;

(b) refuse to register him; or

(c) register him subject to such conditions as the Chief Inspector considers it appropriate to impose.

(6) Conditions imposed under subsection (5)(c) may be conditions applying generally in relation to all cases, or particular classes of case, or such conditions together with specific conditions applying in the particular case.

(7) Where a person is registered subject to conditions imposed under subsection (5)(c), he shall be taken to be authorised to act as a registered inspector only so far as those conditions permit.

(8) The period for which any registration is to have effect shall be determined by the Chief Inspector and shall be entered in the register kept by him.

(9) Nothing in subsection (8) is to be taken as preventing a registered inspector from applying for a fresh registration to take effect immediately on the expiry of his current registration.

11.—(1) If the Chief Inspector is satisfied that any of the conditions mentioned in subsection (2) is satisfied with respect to an inspector registered in his register, he may remove the name of that inspector from that register.

Removal from register and imposition or variation of conditions.

(2) The conditions are that—

    (a) he is no longer a fit and proper person for discharging the functions of a registered inspector under this Act;

    (b) he is no longer capable of conducting inspections under this Act competently and effectively;

    (c) there has been a significant failure on his part to comply with any condition imposed under section 10(5)(c) and subject to which his registration has effect;

    (d) he has knowingly or recklessly produced a report of an inspection which is, in whole or in part, seriously misleading.

(3) If the Chief Inspector is satisfied—

    (a) that he is authorised by subsection (2) to remove the name of an inspector from his register, or

    (b) that it would otherwise be in the public interest to act under this subsection,

he may vary any condition subject to which the registration of that inspector has effect or vary that registration by imposing a condition subject to which it will have effect.

(4) Either Chief Inspector may, in exercising his functions under this section with respect to a registered inspector, have regard to any action taken by the other Chief Inspector with respect to that registered inspector.

12.—(1) Any person who is aggrieved by—

Appeals in relation to registration.

    (a) the refusal of the Chief Inspector to renew his registration under section 10,

    (b) the imposition or variation of any condition subject to which he is registered under that section,

    (c) the removal of his name from the relevant register under section 11,

may appeal against the Chief Inspector's decision to a tribunal constituted in accordance with Schedule 3.

(2) No such decision of the Chief Inspector shall have effect until—

    (a) the disposal of any appeal against it which is duly made under this section; or

    (b) the period within which an appeal may be made has expired without an appeal having been made.

(3) Subsection (2) shall not apply where the Chief Inspector—

    (a) is satisfied that the circumstances of the case are exceptional and justify the decision in question taking effect immediately, or earlier than would otherwise be the case; and

    (b) notifies the person concerned to that effect.

(4) On determining any appeal under this section, the tribunal may—

    (a) confirm, reverse or vary the decision appealed against; or

    (b) remit the case to the Chief Inspector with directions as to the action to be taken by him.

(5) Schedule 3 shall have effect with respect to the tribunals.

Religious education.

13.—(1) This section applies to—

    (a) any voluntary school, and

    (b) any grant-maintained school,

in which denominational education is given to any pupils.

(2) In this section "denominational education" means religious education given otherwise than in accordance with an agreed syllabus.

(3) The school's governing body shall secure that the school's denominational education is inspected under this section.

(4) An inspection under this section shall be conducted by a person chosen by—

    (a) the foundation governors, in the case of a controlled school; and

    (b) the governing body, in any other case.

(5) The person chosen need not be a registered inspector.

(6) Inspections under this section shall be carried out at such intervals as may be prescribed; and in prescribing the intervals the Secretary of State may make provision as to the period within which the first inspection under this section with respect to a school is to begin.

(7) It shall be the general duty of a person conducting an inspection under this section to report on the quality of the denominational education provided by the school for pupils to whom denominational education is given by the school.

(8) A person conducting an inspection under this section may do so with the assistance of such other persons chosen by him as are in his opinion fit and proper persons for carrying out the inspection.

(9) Part II of Schedule 2 makes further provision with respect to inspections under this section.

Provision of inspection services by local education authorities.

14.—(1) Any local education authority may provide a school inspection service for schools within their area.

(2) In this section "school inspection service", in relation to any local education authority, means a service providing for the inspection of schools under section 9 or 13 by officers of the authority.

(3) Any school inspection service provided by a local education authority may, in addition to providing for the inspection of schools which are maintained by them, provide for the inspection of schools which are not maintained by them.

(4) Any school inspection service provided by a local education authority shall be operated by the authority in such a way as can reasonably be expected to secure that the full cost of providing the service is recovered by way of charges made by the authority to those using the service.

(5) The Secretary of State may by regulations—

(a) make provision as to the making of tenders by local education authorities (as required by paragraph 2 of Schedule 2);

(b) make provision with respect to the accounts to be kept by local education authorities in connection with any school inspection services provided by them; and

(c) make such incidental and supplemental provision with respect to school inspection services provided by local education authorities as the Secretary of State considers appropriate.

15.—(1) Where—

(a) a local education authority require information about any matter in connection with a school which is maintained by them, for the purpose of enabling them to exercise any function of theirs, and

(b) it is not reasonably practicable for them to obtain it in any other manner,

they may cause an inspection of the school to be made by one or more of their officers for the purpose of obtaining that information.

Power of local education authority to inspect maintained school for specific purpose.

(2) Any officer of a local education authority inspecting a school under this section shall have at all reasonable times a right of entry to the premises of the school.

Information about schools

16.—(1) The Secretary of State may by regulations make provision requiring the proprietor of each independent school and the governing body of every school which is—

Power of Secretary of State to require information.

(a) maintained by a local education authority,

(b) a grant-maintained school, or

(c) a special school which is not maintained by a local education authority,

to provide such information about the school as may be prescribed.

(2) For the purposes of this section information about the continuing education of pupils leaving a school, or the employment or training taken up by such pupils on leaving, is to be treated as information about the school.

(3) Where the Secretary of State exercises his power to make regulations under this section he shall do so with a view to making available information which is likely to—

(a) assist parents in choosing schools for their children;

(b) increase public awareness of the quality of the education provided by the schools concerned and of the educational standards achieved in those schools; or

(c) assist in assessing the degree of efficiency with which the financial resources of those schools are managed.

(4) Information which is required by virtue of regulations under this section shall be provided—

(a) in such form and manner,

(b) on such occasions, and

(c) to such person or persons, in addition to or in place of the Secretary of State,

as may be prescribed.

(5) No information provided in accordance with regulations under this section shall name any pupil to whom it relates.

(6) The Secretary of State may—

(a) publish information provided in accordance with regulations under this section in such form and manner as he considers appropriate;

(b) make arrangements for such information to be published in such form and manner, and by such persons, as he may specify for the purposes of this section;

(c) make regulations requiring local education authorities to publish prescribed categories of such information, together with such supplementary information as may be prescribed, in such form and manner as may be prescribed.

(7) The Secretary of State may make regulations requiring—

(a) the governing body of any school which is maintained by a local education authority, or which is a grant-maintained school, or

(b) any local education authority,

to provide prescribed persons with prescribed categories of information published under subsection (6).

(8) Information provided under subsection (7) shall be provided in such form and manner as may be prescribed.

(9) Regulations under this section may make provision enabling the Secretary of State, in such circumstances as may be prescribed, to order the deletion from the register of independent schools of the name of any independent school the proprietor of which fails to comply with any requirement imposed by or under the regulations.

(10) This section is not to be taken as restricting, or otherwise affecting, any other powers that the Secretary of State may have to make regulations with respect to, or otherwise to require, the provision of information by any person.

(11) In subsection (9) "the register of independent schools" means—

(a) in relation to any school in England, the register of independent schools kept under section 70 of the Education Act 1944 by the Registrar of Registrar of Independent Schools for England; and

1944 c. 31.

(b) in relation to any school in Wales, the equivalent register kept by the Registrar of Independent Schools for Wales.

(12) This section does not apply to nursery schools.

17. In Part II of the Education (Scotland) Act 1980 (rights and duties of parents and functions of education authorities in relation to individual pupils) after section 28H (appeals relating to exclusion of pupils from schools) there shall be inserted the following sections—

Information as to schools and pupils: Scotland. 1980 c. 44.

"Information as to schools and pupils

Information as to schools.

28I.—(1) The Secretary of State may by regulations make provision requiring—

    (a) in respect of every school for the management of which an education authority is responsible, the education authority; and

    (b) in respect of every other school—

        (i) where the school has a board of management, the board of management;

        (ii) in any other case, the managers,

to provide to him and to such persons (including education authorities) as may be prescribed such information as regards the school and pupils attending the school as may be prescribed.

(2) For the purposes of this section information about the continuing education of pupils leaving a school, or the employment or training taken up by such pupils on leaving, is to be treated as information about the school.

(3) Where the Secretary of State exercises his power to make regulations under this section he shall do so with a view to making available information which is likely to—

    (a) assist parents in choosing schools for their children;

    (b) increase public awareness of the quality of the education provided by the schools concerned and the educational standards achieved in those schools; or

    (c) assist in assessing the degree of efficiency with which the financial resources of those schools are managed.

(4) Information which is required by virtue of regulations made under this section shall be provided—

    (a) in such form and manner; and

    (b) on such occasions,

as may be prescribed.

(5) No information provided in accordance with regulations made under this section shall name any pupil to whom it relates.

(6) The Secretary of State may—

(a) publish information provided in accordance with regulations made under this section in such form and manner as he considers appropriate;

(b) require an education authority to publish such information at such times and in such form and manner as he may specify for the purposes of this section; or

(c) make arrangements for such information to be published in such form and manner, and by such persons, as he may specify for the purposes of this section.

(7) The powers given to the Secretary of State by this section and section 28J of this Act may be exercised so as to make different provision in relation to different areas.

(8) This section and sections 28J and 28K of this Act are not to be taken as restricting, or otherwise affecting, any other powers that the Secretary of State may have to make regulations with respect to, or otherwise require, the provision of information by any person.

(9) Regulations made under this section and sections 28J and 28K of this Act may make different provision for different cases or classes of case.

(10) This section does not apply to nursery schools.

Requirement to provide information as to school education.

28J.—(1) The Secretary of State may make regulations requiring education authorities, boards of management and managers of grant-aided schools to provide to prescribed persons such information or documents or categories of information or documents relating to school education as may be prescribed.

(2) Information or documents provided in pursuance of regulations made under subsection (1) above shall be provided—

(a) in such form and manner; and

(b) on such occasions,

as may be prescribed.

Information as to pupils.

28K.—(1) The Secretary of State may by regulations make provision requiring that such information and reports as may be prescribed as regards pupils attending schools to which this section applies shall be supplied to the parents of such pupils at such times and in such form and manner as may be determined by or in accordance with the regulations.

(2) This section applies to any school which is not a grant-aided school, an independent school or a nursery school.

(3) Regulations made under this section may contain provision as to—

    (a) the means of involvement of parents in consideration of such reports; and

    (b) the extent to which any information relating to general standards of performance in examinations or other forms of assessment of any group of pupils shall be supplied to parents of other pupils."

Miscellaneous

18.—(1) In this Act—

    Interpretation.

"agreed syllabus" has the meaning given in section 114(1) of the Education Act 1944;

    1944 c. 31.

"appropriate authority", in relation to any school, has the meaning given in paragraph 1 of Schedule 2;

"Chief Inspector" shall be read—

    (a) in relation to any school in England, as a reference to Her Majesty's Chief Inspector of Schools in England; and

    (b) in relation to any school in Wales, as a reference to Her Majesty's Chief Inspector of Schools in Wales;

"Chief Inspector for England" has the meaning given in section 1(1);

"Chief Inspector for Wales" has the meaning given in section 5(1);

"city technology college" and "city college for the technology of the arts" have the meanings given in section 105 of the Education Reform Act 1988;

    1988 c. 40.

"delegated budget" has the same meaning as in section 36 of the Education Reform Act 1988;

"denominational education" has the meaning given in section 13(2);

"inspection team" has the meaning given in paragraph 3(1) of Schedule 2;

"maintained school" means any county school, voluntary school, maintained special school, maintained nursery school or grant-maintained school;

"nursery school" has the meaning given in section 9(4) of the Education Act 1944;

"prescribed" means prescribed by regulations made by the Secretary of State; and

"registered inspector" means a person registered under section 10(1) or (2).

(2) For the purposes of this Act any reference to a condition imposed under section 10(5)(c) includes a reference to a condition imposed under section 11(3).

(3) Any person authorised by this Act to inspect records—

    (a) shall be entitled at any reasonable time to have access to, and inspect and check the operation of, any computer and any associated apparatus or material which is or has been in use in connection with the records in question; and

(b) may require—

> (i) the person by whom or on whose behalf the computer is or has been so used; or

> (ii) any person having charge of, or otherwise concerned with the operation of, the computer, apparatus or material,

to afford him such assistance as he may reasonably require.

1944 c. 31.

(4) This Act and the Education Act 1944 shall be construed as one.

Regulations and orders.

19.—(1) In addition to any power to make an Order in Council, any power to make regulations or any other kind of order conferred by this Act shall be exercisable by statutory instrument.

(2) Any statutory instrument containing an order or regulations made under this Act, except one made under section 21(3), shall be subject to annulment in pursuance of a resolution of either House of Parliament.

(3) Any regulations or order made under this Act may make different provision with respect to different cases, or classes of case, (including provision for the designation by the Secretary of State, in accordance with the regulations, of particular schools or classes of school for the purposes of the application of particular provisions of the regulations in relation to such schools) and may make different provision in relation to different areas.

Financial provisions.

20.—(1) There shall be paid out of money provided by Parliament—

(a) any expenses incurred by the Secretary of State under this Act; and

(b) any increase attributable to this Act in the sums payable under any other Act out of money so provided.

(2) There shall be paid into the Consolidated Fund any sums received by the Chief Inspector under section 10(4)(b) or paragraph 4(3) or 5(3) of Schedule 2.

Short title, commencement, extent etc.

21.—(1) This Act may be cited as the Education (Schools) Act 1992.

(2) This Act shall be included among the Acts which may be cited as the Education Acts 1944 to 1992.

(3) Subsections (1) to (6) of this section shall come into force on the passing of this Act but otherwise this Act shall come into force on such date as may be appointed by order made by the Secretary of State.

(4) Subject to subsections (5) and (6), this Act extends to England and Wales only.

(5) Section 17 extends to Scotland only.

(6) Paragraphs 7 to 9 of Schedule 1 and paragraphs 2 and 3 of Schedule 4 also extend to Scotland and Northern Ireland.

(7) The minor and consequential amendments set out in Schedule 4 shall have effect.

(8) The repeals set out in Schedule 5 shall have effect.

SCHEDULES

SCHEDULE 1

HER MAJESTY'S CHIEF INSPECTORS

The Chief Inspectors' other staff

1. The Chief Inspector may, with the approval of the Treasury as to numbers and terms and conditions of service, appoint such staff, in addition to Inspectors who are members of his staff by virtue of section 1(3) or (as the case may be) 5(3), as he thinks fit.

Additional inspectors

2.—(1) The Chief Inspector may arrange for such persons as he thinks fit to assist him in the discharge of any of his functions in relation to a particular case or class of case.

(2) Any person assisting the Chief Inspector under any such arrangements shall be known as an additional inspector.

(3) Any arrangements which provide for assistance by persons who are not members of the Chief Inspector's staff shall be made on terms agreed by him with the Treasury.

(4) An additional inspector acting within the authority conferred on him by the Chief Inspector shall have all the powers of an Inspector.

Remuneration, pensions etc.

3.—(1) There shall be paid to the Chief Inspector such remuneration, and such travelling and other allowances, as the Secretary of State may determine.

(2) In the case of any such Chief Inspector as may be determined by the Secretary of State, there shall be paid such pension, allowance or gratuity to or in respect of him, or such contributions or payments towards provision for such a pension, allowance or gratuity, as may be so determined.

(3) If, when any person ceases to hold office as Chief Inspector, the Secretary of State determines that there are special circumstances which make it right that he should receive compensation, there may be paid to him such sum by way of compensation as may be determined by the Secretary of State.

(4) The approval of the Treasury shall be required for the making of a determination under this paragraph.

(5) Any determination made under this paragraph with respect to one Chief Inspector may be different to any corresponding determination made with respect to the other Chief Inspector.

Expenses of the Chief Inspector and his staff

4. There shall be paid out of money provided by Parliament—

(a) the remuneration of, and any travelling or other allowances payable under this Act to, the Chief Inspector and any staff of his;

(b) any sums payable under this Act to or in respect of the Chief Inspector; and

(c) any expenses duly incurred by the Chief Inspector or by any of his staff in consequence of the provisions of this Act.

Official seal

5. The Chief Inspector shall have an official seal for the authentication of documents required for the purposes of his functions.

Performance of functions

6.—(1) Anything authorised or required by or under this Act or any other enactment to be done by the Chief Inspector for England may be done by—

(a) any of Her Majesty's Inspectors of Schools in England,

(b) any other member of his staff, or

(c) any additional inspector,

who is authorised generally or specially in that behalf by the Chief Inspector for England.

(2) Anything authorised or required by or under this Act or any other enactment to be done by the Chief Inspector for Wales may be done by—

(a) any of Her Majesty's Inspectors of Schools in Wales,

(b) any other member of his staff, or

(c) any additional inspector,

who is authorised generally or specially in that behalf by the Chief Inspector for Wales.

Documentary evidence

1868 c. 37.

7. The Documentary Evidence Act 1868 shall have effect, in relation to the Chief Inspector for England and in relation to the Chief Inspector for Wales, as if—

(a) he were included in the first column of the Schedule to that Act;

(b) he and any person authorised to act on his behalf were mentioned in the second column of that Schedule, and

(c) the regulations referred to in that Act included any document issued by him or by any such person.

The Parliamentary Commissioner

1967 c. 13.

8. In the Parliamentary Commissioner Act 1967, in Schedule 2 (departments and authorities subject to investigation), the following entries shall be inserted at the appropriate places—

"Office of Her Majesty's Chief Inspector of Schools in England."

"Office of Her Majesty's Chief Inspector of Schools in Wales."

Disqualification

1975 c. 24.

9.—(1) In Part III of Schedule 1 to the House of Commons Disqualification Act 1975 (disqualifying offices) the following entries shall be inserted at the appropriate places—

"Her Majesty's Chief Inspector of Schools in England."

"Her Majesty's Chief Inspector of Schools in Wales."

1975 c. 25.

(2) The same entries shall be inserted at the appropriate places in Part III of Schedule 1 to the Northern Ireland Assembly Disqualification Act 1975.

SCHEDULE 2

SCHOOL INSPECTIONS

Sections 9(7) and 13(9).

PART I

INSPECTIONS UNDER SECTION 9

1. In this Part of this Schedule—

"appropriate authority" means—

> (a) in the case of a maintained school (other than a grant-maintained school) whose governing body does not have a delegated budget, the local education authority for that school;

> (b) in the case of a school falling within paragraph (e), (f) or (g) of section 9(3), the proprietor of the school;

> (c) in any other case, the school's governing body; and

"inspection" means an inspection of a school under section 9.

Selection of registered inspectors

2. Before entering into any arrangement for an inspection, the Chief Inspector shall, after consulting the appropriate authority for the school concerned as to the tender specification, invite tenders from at least two registered inspectors who can reasonably be expected—

(a) to wish to tender for the proposed inspection; and

(b) to tender at arm's length from each other.

Inspection teams

3.—(1) Every inspection shall be conducted by a registered inspector with the assistance of a team (an "inspection team") consisting of persons who are fit and proper persons for carrying out the inspection.

(2) It shall be the duty of the registered inspector to ensure that—

(a) at least one member of the inspection team is a person—

> (i) without personal experience in the management of any school or the provision of education in any school (otherwise than as a governor or in any other voluntary capacity); and

> (ii) whose primary function on the team is not that of providing financial or business expertise; and

(b) no member of the inspection team falls within a category of person prescribed for the purposes of this sub-paragraph.

(3) Otherwise, the composition of the inspection team shall be determined by the registered inspector, subject to his complying with any condition imposed under section 10(5)(c).

(4) Any experience of a kind mentioned in sub-paragraph (2)(a) which it is reasonable to regard as insignificant, having regard to the purposes of sub-paragraph (2), may be ignored by the registered inspector.

(5) It shall be the duty of the registered inspector to ensure that no person takes any part in an inspection if he has, or has at any time had, any connection with—

(a) the school in question,

(b) any person who is employed at the school,

(c) any person who is a member of the school's governing body, or

(d) the proprietor of the school,

of a kind which might reasonably be taken to raise doubts about his ability to act impartially in relation to that school.

SCH. 2

Training for inspections

4.—(1) No person shall conduct an inspection of a school in England, or act as a member of an inspection team for such a school, unless he has in the opinion of the Chief Inspector for England, satisfactorily completed a course of training provided by or complying with arrangements approved by that Chief Inspector.

(2) Sub-paragraph (1) shall not apply in such circumstances as may be specified, either generally or in relation to a particular case or class of case, by the Chief Inspector for England.

(3) Where the Chief Inspector for England provides such training he may charge such fees as are reasonable for the purpose of recovering the whole, or part, of the cost of providing it.

5.—(1) No person shall conduct an inspection of a school in Wales, or act as a member of an inspection team for such a school, unless he has in the opinion of the Chief Inspector for Wales, satisfactorily completed a course of training provided by or complying with arrangements approved by that Chief Inspector.

(2) Sub-paragraph (1) shall not apply in such circumstances as may be specified, either generally or in relation to a particular case or class of case, by the Chief Inspector for Wales.

(3) Where the Chief Inspector for Wales provides such training he may charge such fees as are reasonable for the purpose of recovering the whole, or part, of the cost of providing it.

Meeting with parents

6. Where an inspection is arranged, the appropriate authority for the school concerned shall—

    (a) take such steps as are reasonably practicable to notify—

        (i) the parents of registered pupils at the school, and

        (ii) such other persons as may be prescribed,

    of the time when the inspection is to take place; and

    (b) arrange a meeting, in accordance with such provisions as may be prescribed, between the inspector conducting the inspection and those parents of registered pupils at the school who wish to attend.

Rights of entry etc.

7. A registered inspector conducting an inspection, and the members of his inspection team, shall have at all reasonable times—

    (a) a right of entry to the premises of the school concerned; and

    (b) a right to inspect, and take copies of, any records kept by the school, and any other documents containing information relating to the school, which he requires for the purposes of the inspection.

Offence of obstructing inspector or inspection team

8.—(1) It shall be an offence wilfully to obstruct—

    (a) a registered inspector, or

    (b) a member of an inspection team,

in the exercise of his functions in relation to the inspection of a school.

(2) Any person guilty of an offence under sub-paragraph (1) shall be liable on summary conviction to a fine not exceeding level four on the standard scale.

Inspectors' reports

9.—(1) An inspection shall be carried out within such period as may be prescribed.

(2) When an inspection has been completed, the registered inspector shall, before the end of the prescribed period, prepare in writing a report of the inspection and a summary of the report.

(3) The registered inspector shall, without delay, send the report and summary to the appropriate authority for the school concerned and send copies of the report and summary to the Chief Inspector and to—

  (a) the local education authority, in the case of a maintained school (other than a grant-maintained school) for which the governing body are the appropriate authority;

  (b) the governing body (if any), in the case of a maintained school for which the local education authority are the appropriate authority; or

  (c) the Secretary of State, in the case of any other school.

(4) In the case of—

  (a) a voluntary school, or

  (b) a grant-maintained school which was a voluntary school immediately before it became a grant-maintained school,

the registered inspector shall also send a copy of the report and summary to the person who appoints the school's foundation governors.

(5) The appropriate authority shall—

  (a) make any report and summary sent to the authority under sub-paragraph (3) available for inspection by members of the public, at such times and at such a place as may be reasonable;

  (b) provide a copy of the report and summary, free of charge or in prescribed cases on payment of the prescribed fee, to any person who asks for one; and

  (c) take such steps as are reasonably practicable to secure that every parent of a registered pupil at the school receives a copy of the summary as soon as is reasonably practicable.

(6) In addition—

  (a) the governing body of a special school which is not maintained by a local education authority, and

  (b) the proprietor of an independent school approved by the Secretary of State under section 11(3)(a) of the Education Act 1981 (schools suitable for children for whom statements are maintained under section 7 of that Act),

1981 c. 60.

shall, without delay, send a copy of any report and summary sent to the governing body or proprietor under sub-paragraph (3) to any local education authority who are paying fees to the school concerned in respect of a registered pupil at the school.

Action plans

10.—(1) The appropriate authority to whom an inspector has reported under this Part of this Schedule shall, before the end of the prescribed period, prepare a written statement ("the action plan") of the action which they propose to take in the light of his report and the period within which they propose to take it.

(2) Where an action plan has been prepared by an appropriate authority they shall, before the end of the prescribed period, send copies of it to the Chief Inspector and—

(a) where the appropriate authority are the governing body of a maintained school (other than a grant-maintained school), to the local education authority,

(b) where the appropriate authority are the local education authority, to the governing body (if any), or

(c) in any other case, to the Secretary of State,

and to such other persons (if any), in such circumstances, as may be prescribed.

(3) In the case of—

(a) a voluntary school, or

(b) a grant-maintained school which was a voluntary school immediately before it became a grant-maintained school,

the appropriate authority shall also send a copy of the action plan to the person who appoints the school's foundation governors.

(4) In addition—

(a) the governing body of a special school which is not maintained by a local education authority, and

1981 c. 60.

(b) the proprietor of an independent school approved by the Secretary of State under section 11(3)(a) of the Education Act 1981 (schools suitable for children for whom statements are maintained under section 7 of that Act),

shall, without delay, send a copy of any action plan prepared by the governing body or proprietor to any local education authority who are paying fees to the school concerned in respect of a registered pupil at the school.

(5) The appropriate authority shall—

(a) make any action plan prepared by them available for inspection by members of the public, at such times and at such a place as may be reasonable;

(b) provide a copy of the action plan, free of charge or in prescribed cases on payment of the prescribed fee, to any person who asks for one; and

(c) take such steps as are reasonably practicable to secure that every parent of a registered pupil at the school receives a copy of the action plan as soon as is reasonably practicable.

(6) Where the governing body of a maintained school which is not a nursery school have prepared an action plan, they shall include in their governors' report a statement of the extent to which the proposals set out in the action plan have been carried into effect.

(7) In sub-paragraph (6) "governors' report" means—

1988 c. 40.

(a) in the case of a grant-maintained school, the report referred to in section 58(5)(j) of the Education Reform Act 1988; and

1986 c. 61.

(b) in the case of any other kind of maintained school, the report referred to in section 30 of the Education (No.2) Act 1986.

(8) Sub-paragraph (6) applies only in relation to the most recent action plan for the school in question.

Schools considered to be at risk

11.—(1) Where the registered inspector conducting an inspection of a school is of the opinion that the school is failing, or is likely to fail, to give its pupils an acceptable standard of education, he shall express that opinion in his report of the inspection.

(2) The Secretary of State may make regulations with a view to securing that, where such an opinion is expressed in a registered inspector's report, the implementation of the action plan prepared for the school following the report is monitored, in accordance with the provisions of the regulations, by such persons as may be prescribed.

(3) The regulations may, in particular, make provision for reports to be made, by such persons and at such intervals as may be prescribed, with respect to the action taken under the action plan for the school.

Reserve powers of the Chief Inspectors

12.—(1) Where an inspection of a school is required under section 9 but the Chief Inspector is satisfied that it is not reasonably practicable to secure that the school is inspected by a suitable registered inspector, he shall secure that it is inspected—

(a) if it is a school in England, by one of Her Majesty's Inspectors of Schools in England; and

(b) if it is a school in Wales, by one of Her Majesty's Inspectors of Schools in Wales.

(2) Where an inspection is conducted by an Inspector by virtue of this paragraph, the provisions of this Act shall have effect in relation to the inspection as if the Inspector were a registered inspector.

PART II

INSPECTIONS OF DENOMINATIONAL EDUCATION

13. In this Part of this Schedule—

"inspection" means an inspection of a school under section 13; and

"inspector" means the person conducting the inspection.

Inspectors' reports

14.—(1) An inspection shall be carried out within such period as may be prescribed.

(2) When an inspection has been completed, the inspector shall, before the end of the prescribed period, prepare in writing a report of the inspection and a summary of the report.

(3) The inspector shall, without delay, send the report and summary to the governing body for the school concerned.

(4) The governing body shall—

(a) make any such report and its accompanying summary available for inspection by members of the public, at such times and at such a place as may be reasonable;

(b) provide a copy of the report and summary, free of charge or in prescribed cases on payment of the prescribed fee, to any person who asks for one; and

(c) take such steps as are reasonably practicable to secure that every parent of a registered pupil at the school for whom the school provides denominational education receives a copy of the summary as soon as is reasonably practicable.

SCH. 2

Additional action plans

15.—(1) The governing body to whom an inspector has reported under this Part of this Schedule shall, before the end of the prescribed period, prepare a written statement ("the additional action plan") of the action which they propose to take in the light of his report and the period within which they propose to take it.

(2) Where an additional action plan has been prepared by a governing body, they shall, before the end of the prescribed period, send copies of it to the person who appoints the school's foundation governors and—

(a) in the case of a voluntary school, to the local education authority, or

(b) in the case of a grant-maintained school, to the Secretary of State,

and to such other persons (if any), in such circumstances, as may be prescribed.

(3) The governing body shall—

(a) make any additional action plan prepared by them available for inspection by members of the public, at such times and at such a place as may be reasonable;

(b) provide a copy of the plan, free of charge or in prescribed cases on payment of the prescribed fee, to any person who asks for one; and

(c) take such steps as are reasonably practicable to secure that every parent of a registered pupil at the school for whom the school provides denominational education receives a copy of the plan as soon as is reasonably practicable.

(4) Where the governing body of a school have prepared an additional action plan, they shall include in their governors' report a statement of the extent to which the proposals set out in the plan have been carried into effect.

(5) In sub-paragraph (4) "governors' report" means—

1986 c. 61.

(a) in the case of a voluntary school, the report referred to in section 30 of the Education (No. 2) Act 1986; and

1988 c. 40.

(b) in the case of a grant-maintained school, the report referred to in section 58(5)(j) of the Education Reform Act 1988.

(6) Sub-paragraph (4) applies only in relation to the most recent additional action plan for the school in question.

Section 12(5).

SCHEDULE 3

TRIBUNALS HEARING APPEALS UNDER SECTION 12

Constitution of tribunals

1.—(1) A tribunal constituted to hear an appeal under section 12 ("a tribunal") shall consist of—

(a) a Chairman appointed by the Lord Chancellor; and

(b) two other members appointed by the Secretary of State.

1990 c. 41.

(2) To be qualified for appointment as Chairman of a tribunal, a person must have a 7 year general qualification (within the meaning of section 71 of the Courts and Legal Services Act 1990).

Procedure of tribunals

2.—(1) The Secretary of State may by regulations make provision with respect to the making of appeals to, and the procedure to be followed by, tribunals.

(2) The regulations may, in particular, make provision—

  (a) as to the period within which, and manner in which, appeals must be brought;

  (b) for the holding of hearings in private in prescribed circumstances;

  (c) as to the persons who may appear on behalf of the parties;

  (d) for enabling hearings to be conducted even though a member of the tribunal, other than the Chairman, is absent;

  (e) as to the disclosure by the appellant, and others, of documents and the inspection of documents;

  (f) requiring persons to attend the proceedings and give evidence;

  (g) as to the payment of expenses incurred by persons compelled to attend proceedings by regulations made by virtue of paragraph (f);

  (h) authorising the administration of oaths to witnesses;

  (i) as to the withdrawal of appeals;

  (j) as to costs and expenses incurred by any party to the proceedings; and

  (k) authorising preliminary or incidental matters in relation to an appeal to be dealt with by the Chairman of the tribunal hearing that appeal.

Staff

3.—(1) The Secretary of State may, with the consent of the Treasury, make such provision as he thinks fit for—

  (a) the allocation of staff for any tribunal;

  (b) the remuneration of members of tribunals and the reimbursement of their expenses;

  (c) defraying any reasonable expenses incurred by any tribunal.

(2) Any sums payable under any provision made by the Secretary of State under sub-paragraph (1) shall be paid out of money provided by Parliament.

SCHEDULE 4   Section 21(7).

MINOR AND CONSEQUENTIAL AMENDMENTS

The Education Act 1944 (c. 31)

1. In section 77(1) of the Education Act 1944 (inspection of educational establishments)—

  (a) the words "a school" shall be omitted; and

  (b) for "which is not" there shall be substituted "which is neither a school nor".

The Tribunals and Inquiries Act 1971 (c. 62)

2. In section 13(1) of the Tribunals and Inquiries Act 1971 (appeals from certain tribunals), after "6(a)" there shall be inserted "or (d)".

3. In paragraph 6 of Part I of Schedule 1 to the Act of 1971 (tribunals under direct supervision of Council), after sub-paragraph (c) there shall be inserted the following sub-paragraph—

    "(d) a tribunal constituted in accordance with Schedule 3 to the Education (Schools) Act 1992."

The Education Act 1980 (c. 20)

4.—(1) In section 8 of the Education Act 1980 (information as to schools and admission arrangements), the following subsections shall be substituted for subsections (5) and (6)—

"(5) The governors of each school maintained by a local education authority—

    (a) shall publish such information as respects that school as may be required by regulations made by the Secretary of State; and

    (b) may publish such other information with respect to the school as they think fit.

(5A) For the purposes of this section information about the continuing education of pupils leaving a school, or the employment or training taken up by such pupils on leaving, is to be treated as information about the school.

(5B) Every local education authority shall publish such information as may be required by regulations made by the Secretary of State with respect to their policy and arrangements in respect of any matter relating to primary or secondary education in their area.

(6) A local education authority may, with the agreement of the governors of any school maintained by the authority, publish on behalf of the governors the particulars or information relating to the school which are referred to in subsection (2) or (5) above."

(2) In section 9 of the Act of 1980 (nursery schools and special schools) in subsection (2), for "(5) and (7)" there shall be substituted "(5) to (7)".

The Education (No. 2) Act 1986 (c. 6)

5. In section 30 of the Education (No. 2) Act 1986 (governors' annual report to parents in case of county, voluntary and maintained special schools), the following subsection shall be added at the end—

"(5) The Secretary of State may by order make such amendments of subsection (2) above as he considers expedient."

The Education Reform Act 1988 (c. 40)

6.—(1) Section 22 of the Education Reform Act 1988 (provision of information) shall be amended as follows.

(2) In subsection (2), the following shall be added at the end—

"; and

    (d) the educational achievements of pupils at such categories of school as may be prescribed (including results of the kind mentioned in paragraph (c))."

(3) In subsection (5), the following paragraphs shall be inserted after paragraph (a)—

"(aa) the pupil concerned;

    (ab) in the case of a pupil who has transferred to a different school, the head teacher of that school;".

(4) In subsection (5), in the words following paragraph (c)—

    (a) after "governing body" there shall be inserted "the head teacher"; and

    (b) the words "by that body or authority" shall be omitted.

7. In section 226 of the Act of 1988 (services for schools in other member States providing education for British children), in subsection (2)(b), for the words from "school" to the end of the paragraph there shall be substituted "by, or under the direction of, one or more of Her Majesty's Inspectors of Schools for England". SCH. 4

SCHEDULE 5

REPEALS

Section 21(8).

Chapter	Short title	Extent of repeal
7 & 8 Geo. 6. c. 31.	The Education Act 1944.	In section 77, in subsection (1), the words "a school", and subsections (5) and (6).
1988 c. 40.	The Education Reform Act 1988.	In section 22, in subsection (2), the second "and" and in subsection (5) the words "by that body or authority". In Schedule 1, paragraph 5.

PRINTED IN THE UNITED KINGDOM BY PAUL FREEMAN
Controller and Chief Executive of Her Majesty's Stationery Office
and Queen's Printer of Acts of Parliament

HMSO publications are available from:

HMSO Publications Centre
(Mail, fax and telephone orders only)
PO Box 276, London SW8 5DT
Telephone orders 071-873 9090
General enquiries 071-873 0011
(queuing system in operation for both numbers)
Fax orders 071-873 8200

HMSO Bookshops
49 High Holborn, London WC1V 6HB   071-873 0011 (Counter service only)
258 Broad Street, Birmingham B1 2HE   021-643 3740
Southey House, 33 Wine Street, Bristol BS1 2BQ   (0272) 264306
9-21 Princess Street, Manchester M60 8AS   061-834 7201
80 Chichester Street, Belfast BT1 4JY   (0232) 238451
71 Lothian Road, Edinburgh EH3 9AZ   031-228 4181

HMSO's Accredited Agents
(see Yellow Pages)

And through good booksellers

LONDON: HMSO
£4.65 net

ISBN 0-10-543892-8